SEE HABIT AS A GIFT FROM GOD.

──➤➢-◉-≼⋘──

❑ A *Habit* Is Any Action, Conduct Or Behavior That You Do Over And Over Again. It may be a *bad* habit like smoking, or a *good* habit like brushing your teeth.

❑ This means *anything you do twice becomes easier.* It is God's way of helping you *succeed.*

❑ Some experts believe that when you do a specific thing repeatedly 21 consecutive days, it will become a lifetime habit for you.

══════════ ***The Word*** ══════════
"Every good gift and every perfect gift is from above, and cometh down from the Father of lights, with Whom is no variableness, neither shadow of turning." (James 1:17)

2

MAKE A LIST OF NEW HABITS.

❑ Brainstorm For *New* Habits. Make up your bed *immediately* upon rising. Use a highlighter pen to mark your Bible each day.

❑ Hang up your clothes. Make a daily "to-do" list each morning. Limit each phone call to five minutes.

❑ Rise the *same time* every morning. Keep an Idea Notebook with you at *all times*. Write at least one sentence in your daily diary or journal.

The Word

"Write the vision, and make it plain upon the tables, that he may run that readeth it." (Hab. 2:2)

3

EXAMINE SUCCESS HABITS OF CHAMPIONS.

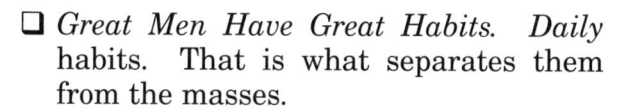

- *Great Men Have Great Habits. Daily* habits. That is what separates them from the masses.

- Men do not really decide their future. They merely decide their habits. Then... their *habits* decide their future.

- Read biographies of champions. *The secret of their success is always hidden in something they do DAILY.*

The Word

"Now when Daniel knew that the writing was signed, he went into his house; and his windows being open in his chamber toward Jerusalem, he kneeled upon his knees three times a day, and prayed and gave thanks before his God, as he did aforetime."

(Dan. 6:10)

4
NAME THE HABITS YOU MOST DESIRE.

❏ Take a sheet of paper. *List* those habits that make men unusually successful. Specify those habits that could apply to *your* life and help you achieve your goals.

❏ Target *one* new habit this week. Now, believe that God will help you achieve it.

5
BEGIN A GOOD HABIT TODAY.

❏ *Decide To Change.* Make a change in something you do every day. *You will never really change your life until you change something you do daily.*

❏ *Choose* to develop the habits of champions. *Start a new one today.*

The Word
"Therefore if any man be in Christ, he is a new creature: old things are passed away; behold all things are become new." (2 Cor. 5:17)

6

ALLOW YOURSELF TIME TO CHANGE.

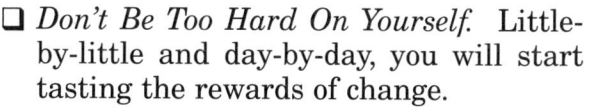

- *Don't Be Too Hard On Yourself.* Little-by-little and day-by-day, you will start tasting the rewards of change.

- Look at the patience of God with Israel. He "knew they were but flesh." He took many years to even train their leader, Moses. You are not an exception.

- Every man fails. Champions simply get back up...and *begin again.*

The Word

"The Lord upholdeth all that fall, and raiseth up all those that be bowed down." (Ps. 145:14)

7

CONFRONT DESTRUCTIVE HABITS.

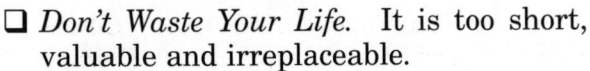

- *Don't Waste Your Life.* It is too short, valuable and irreplaceable.

- Confront problems. *What You Refuse To Master Today, Will Master You Tomorrow.*

- Remember—*What You Do Habitually Determines What You Become Permanently.* Get up. Fight back. You can *win*.

The Word

"Submit yourselves therefore to God. Resist the devil, and he will flee from you." (James 4:7)

~ 8 ~

DO NOT DECEIVE YOURSELF.

❑ *You Already Know The Bad Habits In Your Life.* Face them. *You Will Never Correct What You Are Unwilling To Confront.*

❑ Resist the urge to justify yourself. *Truth Is Temporarily Painful, But Permanently Liberating.*

❑ Change is possible. Step-by-step and day-by-day, start moving toward the dreams and goals of your life.

The Word

"Search me, O God, and know my heart: try me, and know my thoughts: And see if there be any wicked way in me, and lead me in the way everlasting."

(Ps. 139:23,24)

9

DESPISE YOUR CHAINS.

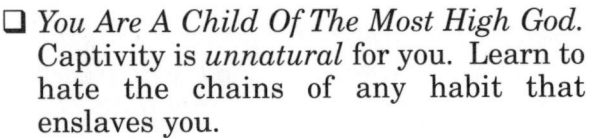

- *You Are A Child Of The Most High God.* Captivity is *unnatural* for you. Learn to hate the chains of any habit that enslaves you.

- While drug addicts and alcoholics may want the *taste* of sin, they certainly do not want the *torment*. But they will never be free until they learn to *despise* those chains.

- Habit is hell's greatest weapon in destroying your life. *Let God break your chains.*

The Word

"The Spirit of the Lord God is upon me; because the Lord hath anointed me to preach good tidings unto the meek; He hath sent me to bind up the brokenhearted, to proclaim liberty to the captives, and the opening of the prison to them that are bound." (Isa. 61:1)

"If the Son therefore shall make you free, ye shall be free indeed.' (Jn. 8:36)

≈ 10 ≈

DIFFERENTIATE BETWEEN DISCIPLINE AND HABIT.

❑ *Many People Do Not Know The Difference Between Discipline And Habit.*

❑ Discipline is forcing yourself to do something. It may be uncomfortable, unpleasant, even miserable in the beginning. *It Is Simply Doing Something You Hate, To Create Something You Love.*

❑ Habit is the child of discipline. It is something you do *naturally,* easily and without conscious effort. Champions become champions by *maintaining a discipline until it becomes a habit,* a daily routine in their lives.

=== ***The Word*** ===

"Evening, and morning, and at noon, will I pray, and cry aloud; and He shall hear my voice." (Ps. 55:17)

≈ 11 ≈

PINPOINT YOUR LIFE-PURPOSE.

❏ Great Habits Are The Results Of Great *Purpose*.

❏ Let me explain. Mohammed Ali, the famous boxer, felt he was divinely appointed to become the heavyweight champion of the world. He felt he was born for *such a purpose*. This sense of purpose was his motivation to develop the daily workout *habits* that made him great.

❏ Always remember the powerful importance of *linking your habits to your life-purpose*.

The Word

"But ye are a chosen generation, a royal priesthood, an holy nation, a peculiar people; that ye should shew forth the praises of Him Who hath called you out of darkness into His marvellous light."

(1 Pet. 2:9)

12

PERFECT YOUR DAILY SUCCESS ROUTINE.

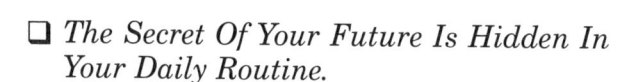

❑ *The Secret Of Your Future Is Hidden In Your Daily Routine.*

❑ Daily tasks should be performed at the *same time* each day. Weekly tasks should be performed on the *same day* each week. Develop a *rhythm* to your life.

❑ Sit down now. Make your personal list of daily activities. Link each task to a specific time or day to be performed.

The Word
"And He came to Nazareth, where He had been brought up: and, *as His custom was,* He went into the synagogue on the sabbath day, and stood up for to read."
(Lk. 4:16)

≈ 13 ≈

EXERCISE EVERY DAY.

- *Health Is Life's First Prize.* Good *health* is a product of good habits.

- *Make the effort.* Schedule 30 minutes each day for exercise. Take care of your body, and it will take care of you.

- Ask your close friends to help motivate you. Set achievable goals. *Just do it. TODAY.*

The Word
"What? know ye not that your body is the temple of the Holy Ghost which is in you, which ye have of God and ye are not your own? For ye are bought with a price: therefore glorify God in your body, and in your spirit, which are God's."

(1 Cor. 6:19,20)

14

ATTEND CHURCH FAITHFULLY.

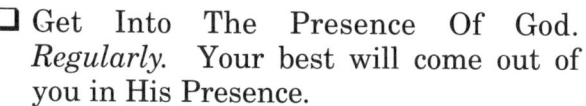

- ❑ Get Into The Presence Of God. *Regularly*. Your best will come out of you in His Presence.

- ❑ Sit under the teaching of a man of God you respect. Put your time, influence and finances there. *Faithfully*.

- ❑ Even Jesus attended church regularly. There is no substitute for the Golden Link of Godly relationships.

The Word

"Not forsaking the assembling of ourselves together, as the manner of some is; but exhorting one another: and so much the more, as ye see the day approaching." (Heb. 10:25)
"...as His custom was, He went into the synagogue on the sabbath day."
(Lk. 4:16)

15

BEGIN THE BIBLE HABIT.

❏ Pick a time...preferably, the *morning*. Call it your "Wisdom-Hour." *Read the Bible aloud.*

❏ Do not get bogged down in theology, or the Greek and Hebrew translations. Just *meditate* on His Word.

❏ His Word is *life*. His Word creates *faith*. His Word will *change the course of your life*.

The Word
"Study to shew thyself approved unto God, a workman that needeth not to be ashamed, rightly dividing the word of truth. But shun profane and vain babblings: for they will increase unto more ungodliness." (2 Tim. 2:15,16)

16

TITHE HABITUALLY.

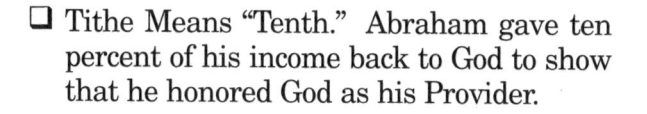

- Tithe Means "Tenth." Abraham gave ten percent of his income back to God to show that he honored God as his Provider.

- His son Isaac tithed also and reaped one hundredfold the same year he sowed. God rewarded his Seed.

- Think like a sower. Your Seed is anything you give to God. Your Harvest is anything He gives back to you. *Habitual Sowing Guarantees Habitual Reaping.*

The Word

"Bring ye all the tithes into the storehouse, that there may be meat in Mine house, and prove Me now herewith, saith the Lord of hosts, if I will not open you the windows of heaven, and pour you out a blessing, that there shall not be room enough to receive it." (Mal. 3:10)

"Upon the first day of the week let every one of you lay by him in store, as God hath prospered him." (1 Cor. 16:2)

17

DEVELOP THE INFORMATION HABIT.

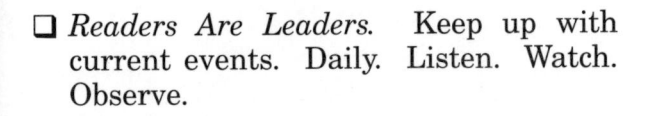

- *Readers Are Leaders.* Keep up with current events. Daily. Listen. Watch. Observe.

- Ask questions. Analyze what happens around you. Open your eyes. Become aware. *Make it a habit.*

- *Ignorance Creates Crisis.* Information solves it.

The Word

"My people are destroyed for lack of knowledge: because thou hast rejected knowledge, I will also reject thee."
(Hos. 4:6)

"...but through knowledge shall the just be delivered." (Prov. 11:9)

~ 18 ~

PRACTICE POWER-TALK.

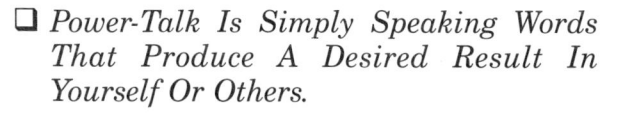

- *Power-Talk Is Simply Speaking Words That Produce A Desired Result In Yourself Or Others.*

- Champions *talk* differently. They discuss their future, not their past; their victories, not their defeats. *Never say anything you don't want another to believe.* Start saying what God says about your life.

- Words create pictures in your mind. Those pictures decide what you believe. *What You Look At The Longest Will Affect You The Most.*

The Word

"Death and life are in the power of the tongue: and they that love it shall eat the fruit thereof." (Prov. 18:21)

~ 19 ~

AVOID ANYONE WHO BREAKS YOUR FOCUS.

- *The Only Reason Men Fail Is Broken Focus.* It happened with Samson and Delilah. It happened with David and Bathsheba. Do not let it happen to you.

- Satan dreads your total concentration on God's Assignment in your life.

- *When Satan Wants To Destroy You, He Sends A Person Into Your Life.*

The Word

"Be not deceived: evil communications corrupt good manners." (1 Cor. 15:33)
"For the Lord giveth wisdom...to deliver thee from the way of the evil man...to deliver thee from the strange woman." (Prov. 2:6,12,16)

20

GET ENOUGH SLEEP.

- *When Fatigue Walks In, Faith Walks Out.*

- When you are tired, you *change.* you *talk* differently, you *think* differently, you *assess* life differently. And *always inaccurately.*

- Accept your personal and unique sleep requirements. Make a habit of going to bed every night at the same time. Your life depends on it.

The Word
"And He said unto them, Come ye yourselves apart into a desert place, and rest a while: for there were many coming and going, and they had not leisure so much as to eat." (Mk. 6:31)

21

SET A SPECIFIC PRAYER TIME.

❏ *Setting A Specific Prayer Time Is One Of The Great Secrets In The Lives Of Prayer Champions.*

❏ Build your daily agenda around your specific prayer time. *Morning* is usually best. Make it the *priority* of the day.

❏ You will be amazed at the power of keeping a *daily appointment* with God.

The Word
"My voice shalt thou hear in the morning, O Lord; in the morning will I direct my prayer unto Thee, and will look up." (Ps. 5:3)

≈ 22 ≈

LINK TWO GREAT HABITS TOGETHER.

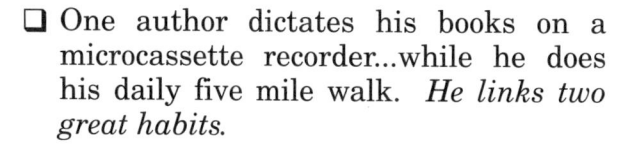

- ❑ One author dictates his books on a microcassette recorder...while he does his daily five mile walk. *He links two great habits.*

- ❑ Some keep an *Idea Notebook* handy during their prayer time. This enables them to easily document ideas fresh from God.

- ❑ You can do the same. Build on the good habits you already have.

The Word
"For precept must be upon precept, precept upon precept; line upon line, line upon line: here a little, and there a little." (Isa. 28:10)

23

MOVE TOWARD ORDER.

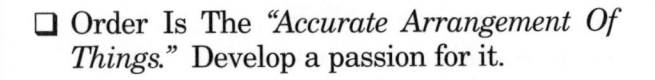

- ❏ Order Is The *"Accurate Arrangement Of Things."* Develop a passion for it.

- ❏ You do not park your car in your bedroom. You do not sleep on your kitchen table. You hang your clothes in your closet. You brush your teeth at the bathroom sink. *Order is doing the right thing...at the right time...in the right place.*

- ❏ Order increases productivity. Your productivity increases your contribution. Your contribution increases the rewards you receive in life.

=== *The Word* ===

"And God saw every thing that He had made, and, behold, it was very good. And the evening and the morning were the sixth day. Thus the heavens and the earth were finished, and all the host of them. And on the seventh day God ended His work which He hath made."

(Gen. 1:31, 2:1,2)

24

PRACTICE THE E.H.A.H. SYSTEM.

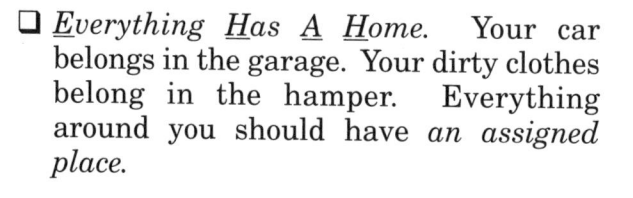

- *Everything Has A Home.* Your car belongs in the garage. Your dirty clothes belong in the hamper. Everything around you should have *an assigned place.*

- *Everything Has A Home.* Insist on it. Make certain everything is *returned* to its assigned place.

- *Everything Has A Home.* This explains the incredible secret of *Order*. It is the secret of great *productivity*.

The Word
"Let all things be done decently and in order." (1 Cor. 14:40)
"To every thing there is a season, and a time to every purpose under the heaven." (Eccl. 3:1)

25

RECOGNIZE THE LAW OF EVENTUALITY.

- ❑ If you smoke three packs of cigarettes a day, what is the *inevitable eventuality?* If you eat two slices of pecan pie late every night, what is the *inevitable eventuality?*

- ❑ This is the difference between champions and losers. *Losers* make decisions that create their desired *present. Champions* make the decisions that create their desired *future.*

- ❑ *Your daily habits are carving out an irreversible future.* Are you heading toward *what you really want?*

The Word
"Be not deceived; God is not mocked: for whatsoever a man soweth, that shall he also reap." (Gal. 6:7)

~ 26 ~

SOW FROM EVERY PAYCHECK.

❏ You Want To *Receive Regularly...Sow Regularly.*

❏ Start the habit of giving something to the work of God out of every paycheck you receive. When you sow consistently, you will reap consistently.

❏ Expect God to multiply your Seed one hundredfold as He promised clearly in Mark 10:30. *He will provide Seed to anyone willing to sow it.*

The Word

"Now He that ministereth seed to the sower both minister bread for your food, and multiply your seed sown, and increase the fruits of your righteousness;" (2 Cor. 9:10)
"While the earth remaineth, seedtime and harvest,...shall not cease."

(Gen. 8:22)

~ 27 ~

DECIDE YOUR DESTINATION.

❏ What You Are Doing *Today Is Creating A Permanent* You.

❏ *Your habits are vehicles*...taking you into a desirable or undesirable future. Where will your present habits take you in 12 months? In 10 years?

❏ *Where will you eventually be if you do not change the direction you are going?* Will you require a tragedy to initiate a change?

The Word
"I call heaven and earth to record this day against you, that I have set before you life and death, blessing and cursing: therefore choose life, that both thou and thy seed may live:" (Deut. 30:19)
"Be not deceived; God is not mocked: for whatsoever a man soweth, that shall he also reap." (Gal. 6:7)

28

ESTABLISH GOOD FAMILY HABITS.

- Suzanne Wesley had seventeen children. She habitually set aside the first day each month to devote total attention to her oldest child. Day two was spent on her second child, and so forth. This may explain the greatness of her son, John Wesley.

- *Great families usually have great habits.* Follow daily and weekly habits that will create the family unit you desire.

- *Designate one night a week as family night.* Cherish it. Build your weekly agenda around it.

The Word
"And if it seem evil unto you to serve the Lord, choose you this day whom ye will serve;...but as for me and my house, we will serve the Lord." (Josh. 24:15)

29

MOVE TOWARD EXTRAORDINARY PEOPLE.

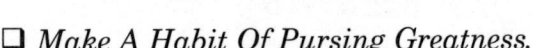

- *Make A Habit Of Pursing Greatness.*

- Elisha received a double-portion of God's power because he was willing to pay any price to *stay in the presence* of Elijah, the great prophet.

- Joshua observed Moses. Ruth reached for Boaz. *You Will Never Possess What You Are Unwilling To Pursue.*

The Word
"He that walketh with wise men shall be wise: but a companion of fools shall be destroyed." (Prov. 13:20)

30

REMEMBER... SUCCESS IS A DAILY EVENT.

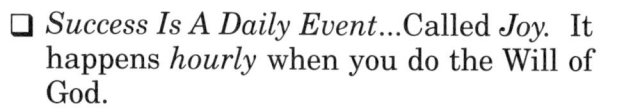

- *Success Is A Daily Event*...Called *Joy*. It happens *hourly* when you do the Will of God.

- *Habit* is also a daily thing. *Nothing Will Ever Dominate Your Life Unless It Happens Daily.*

- *Focus* on *today's* priorities. *A priority is anything God has commanded you to do today.*

The Word

"It is of the Lord's mercies that we are not consumed, because His compassions fail not. They are new every morning: great is Thy faithfulness."

(Lam. 3:22,23)

31

EXPECT GOD TO HELP YOU.

- *You Are Not Alone.* Somebody is committed to your success. *God really does care.* He is your *Enabler.*

- He created you *for a purpose.* His Holy Spirit will break the bondage of your bad habits. He will also give you the power to birth the *right* habits.

- Ask for the gift of the Holy Spirit. When He comes, He will lead you into all truth. *There is no other road of deliverance.*

The Word

"But ye shall receive power, after that the Holy Ghost is come upon you: and ye shall be witnesses unto Me both in Jerusalem, and in all Judaea, and in Samaria, and unto the uttermost part of the earth." (Acts 1:8)

DECISION PAGE

Will You Accept Jesus As Your Personal Savior Today?

The Bible says, "That if thou shalt confess with thy mouth the Lord Jesus, and shalt believe in thine heart that God hath raised Him from the dead, thou shalt be saved" (Rom. 10:9).

Pray this prayer from your heart today!

"Dear Jesus, I believe that You died for me and rose again on the third day. I confess I am a sinner...I need Your love and forgiveness...Come into my heart. Forgive my sins. I receive Your eternal life. Confirm Your love by giving me peace, joy and supernatural love for others. Amen."

Return this today!

☐ Yes, Mike! I made a decision to accept Christ as my personal Savior today. Please send me my free gift of your book, *"31 Keys To A New Beginning"* to help me with my new life in Christ. *(B-48)*

NAME		BIRTHDAY
ADDRESS		
CITY	STATE	ZIP
PHONE	E-MAIL	*B-18*

(Clip and Mail)

Mail Form To:
The Wisdom Center · P. O. Box 99 · Denton, TX 76202
1-888-WISDOM-1 (1-888-947-3661)
Website: ***www.thewisdomcenter.cc***

Unless otherwise indicated, all Scripture quotations are taken from the King James Version of the Bible.
Seeds Of Wisdom On Habits · ISBN 1-56394-085-X
Copyright © 2001 by *MIKE MURDOCK*
All publishing rights belong exclusively to Wisdom International
Published by The Wisdom Center · P.O. Box 99 · Denton, TX 76202
1-888-WISDOM-1 (1-888-947-3661) · Website:www.thewisdomcenter.cc
Printed in the United States of America. All rights reserved under International Copyright Law. Contents and/or cover may not be reproduced in whole or in part in any form without the express written consent of the publisher.

ABOUT *MIKE MURDOCK*

- Has embraced his Assignment to pursue...possess...and publish the Wisdom of God to help people achieve their dreams and goals.

- Began full-time evangelism at the age of 19, which has continued since 1966.

- Has traveled and spoken to more than 14,000 audiences in 38 countries, including East and West Africa, the Orient, and Europe.

- Noted author of 130 books, including best sellers, *"Wisdom For Winning," "Dream Seeds"* and *"The Double Diamond Principle."*

- Created the popular *"Topical Bible"* series for Businessmen, Mothers, Fathers, Teenagers, and the *"One-Minute Pocket Bible"* series and *"The Uncommon Life"* series.

- Has composed more than 5,700 songs such as *"I Am Blessed," "You Can Make It,"* "Holy Spirit This Is Your House" and *"Jesus, Just The Mention Of Your Name,"* recorded by many gospel artists.

- Is the Founder of The Wisdom Center, in Denton Texas.

- Has a weekly television program called *"Wisdom Keys With Mike Murdock."*

- Has appeared often on TBN, CBN, and other television network programs.

- Is a Founding Trustee on the Board of Charismatic Bible Ministries with Oral Roberts.

- Has had more than 3,500 accept the call into full-time ministry under his ministry.

WISDOM 12 PAK

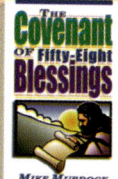

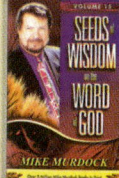

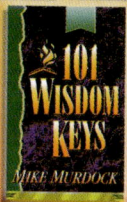

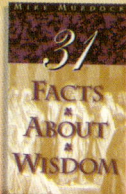

1. MY PERSONAL DREAM BOOK - B143 - $5.00
2. THE COVENANT OF FIFTY-EIGHT BLESSINGS - B47 - $8.00
3. WISDOM, GOD'S GOLDEN KEY TO SUCCESS - B71 - $7.00
4. SEEDS OF WISDOM ON THE HOLY SPIRIT - B116 - $5.00
5. SEEDS OF WISDOM ON THE SECRET PLACE - B115 - $5.00
6. SEEDS OF WISDOM ON THE WORD OF GOD - B117 - $5.00
7. SEEDS OF WISDOM ON YOUR ASSIGNMENT - B122 - $5.00
8. SEEDS OF WISDOM ON PROBLEM SOLVING - B118 - $5.00
9. 101 WISDOM KEYS - B45 - $7.00
10. 31 KEYS TO A NEW BEGINNING - B48 - $7.00
11. THE PROVERBS 31 WOMAN - B49 - $7.00
12. 31 FACTS ABOUT WISDOM - B46 - $7.00

Wisdom Is The Principal Thing
Book Pak WBL-12 / $30
(A $73 Value!)
The Wisdom Center

ORDER TODAY! 1-888-WISDOM-1
www.thewisdomcenter.cc (1-888-947-3661)

THE WISDOM CENTER • P.O. Box 99 • Denton, TX 76202

Money Matters.

This Powerful Video will unleash the Financial Harvest of your lifetime!

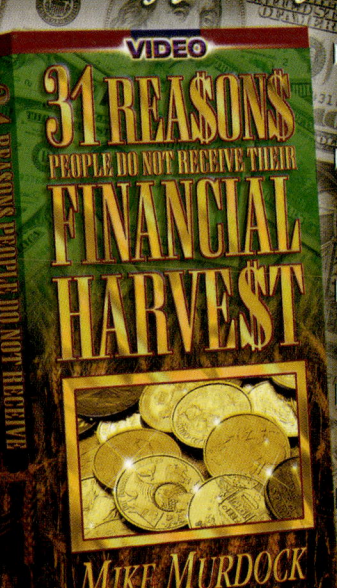

- 8 Scriptural Reasons You Should Pursue Financial Prosperity
- The Secret Prayer Key You Need When Making A Financial Request To God
- The Weapon Of Expectation And The 5 Miracles It Unlocks
- How To Discern Those Who Qualify To Receive Your Financial Assistance
- How To Predict The Miracle Moment God Will Schedule Your Financial Breakthrough

Wisdom Is The Principal Thing
Video VI-17 / $30
Six Audio Tapes / $30 TS-71
Book / $12 B-82
The Wisdom Center

ORDER TODAY! 1-888-WISDOM-1
www.thewisdomcenter.cc (1-888-947-3661)

THE WISDOM CENTER • P.O. Box 99 • Denton, TX 76202

The Secret To 1000 Times More.

In this Dynamic Video you will find answers to unleash Financial Flow into your life!

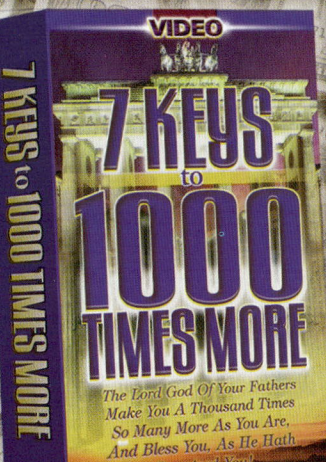

- Habits Of Uncommon Achievers
- The Greatest Success Law I Ever Discovered
- How To Discern Your Place Of Assignment, The Only Place Financial Provision Is Guaranteed
- 3 Secret Keys In Solving Problems For Others
- How To Become The Next Person To Receive A Raise On Your Job

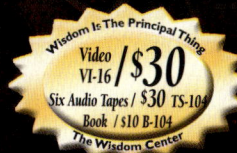

Wisdom Is The Principal Thing
Video VI-16 / $30
Six Audio Tapes / $30 TS-104
Book / $10 B-104
The Wisdom Center

ORDER TODAY! **1-888-WISDOM-1**
www.thewisdomcenter.cc (1-888-947-3661)

THE WISDOM CENTER • P.O. Box 99 • Denton, TX 76202

Somebody's Future Will Not Begin Until You Enter.

THE ASSIGNMENT: THE ANOINTING & THE ADVERSITY — MIKE MURDOCK

THE ASSIGNMENT: THE DREAM & THE DESTINY — MIKE MURDOCK

THE ASSIGNMENT: THE PAIN & THE PASSION — MIKE MURDOCK

THE ASSIGNMENT: THE TRIALS & THE TRIUMPHS — MIKE MURDOCK

THIS COLLECTION INCLUDES 4 DIFFERENT BOOKS CONTAINING UNCOMMON WISDOM FOR DISCOVERING YOUR LIFE ASSIGNMENT

- How To Achieve A God-Given Dream And Goal
- How To Know Who Is Assigned To You
- The Purpose And Rewards Of An Enemy

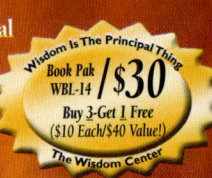

Wisdom Is The Principal Thing
Book Pak WBL-14 / **$30**
Buy 3-Get 1 Free
($10 Each/$40 Value!)
The Wisdom Center

ORDER TODAY! 1-888-WISDOM-1
www.thewisdomcenter.cc (1-888-947-3661)

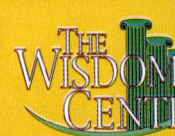

THE WISDOM CENTER • P.O. Box 99 • Denton, TX 76202

THE SECRET.

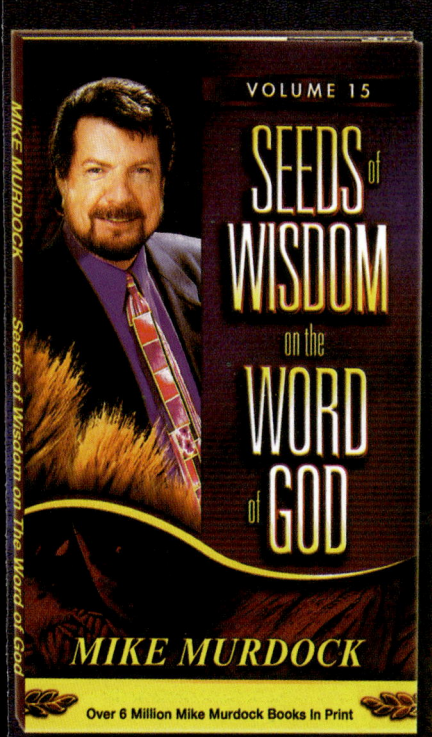

- 11 Reasons Why The Bible Is The Most Important Book On Earth
- 12 Problems The Word Of God Can Solve In Your Life
- 4 Of My Personal Bible Reading Secrets
- 4 Steps To Building A Spiritual Home
- 9 Wisdom Keys To Being Successful In Developing The Habit Of Reading The Word Of God

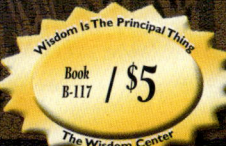

Book B-117 / $5

ORDER TODAY! 1-888-WISDOM-1
www.thewisdomcenter.cc (1-888-947-3661)

THE WISDOM CENTER • P.O. Box 99 • Denton, TX 76202

Your Assignment Is Your Discovery, Not Your Decision.

- **11 Seasons Of Preparation For Your Assignment**
- **6 Rewards Of Pain**
- **6 Keys For Developing An Obsession For Your Assignment**
- **3 Wisdom Keys To Turning Your Anger Into Passion For Your Assignment**

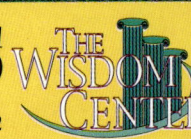

Wisdom Is The Principal Thing
Book B-122 / $5
The Wisdom Center

ORDER TODAY! 1-888-WISDOM-1
www.thewisdomcenter.cc (1-888-947-3661)

THE WISDOM CENTER • P.O. Box 99 • Denton, TX 76202

WISDOM COLLECTION
8

SECRETS OF THE UNCOMMON MILLIONAIRE

1. The Uncommon Millionaire Conference Vol. 1 (Six Cassettes)
2. The Uncommon Millionaire Conference Vol. 2 (Six Cassettes)
3. The Uncommon Millionaire Conference Vol. 3 (Six Cassettes)
4. The Uncommon Millionaire Conference Vol. 4 (Six Cassettes)
5. 31 Reasons People Do Not Receive Their Financial Harvest (256 Page Book)
6. Secrets of the Richest Man Who Ever Lived (178 Page Book)
7. 12 Seeds Of Wisdom Books On 12 Topics
8. The Gift Of Wisdom For Leaders Desk Calendar
9. 101 Wisdom Keys On Tape (Audio Tape)
10. In Honor Of The Holy Spirit (Music Cassette)
11. 365 Memorization Scriptures On The Word Of God (Audio Cassette)

Wisdom Is The Principal Thing
THE WISDOM COLLECTION 8
SECRETS OF THE UNCOMMON MILLIONAIRE
WC-08 / $195
The Wisdom Center

ORDER TODAY! 1-888-WISDOM-1
www.thewisdomcenter.cc (1-888-947-3661)

THE WISDOM CENTER • P.O. Box 99 • Denton, TX 76202

The Secrets For Surviving.

- How To Get Through The Storms Of Your Life!
- Avoiding the #1 Trap Satan Uses Against Believers!
- Keys To Discovering Wrong People In Your Life!
- Satan's 3 Most Effective Weapons!
- How To Use Adversity A Stepping Stone To Wisdom!
- How To Stand When Everything Is Falling Apart!
- Six Seasons Satan Always Attacks You!
- Battle Techniques Of War-Weary Saints!
- Reversing Satanic Strategy!
- How To Get Back Up When The Devil Puts You Down!

Six Wisdom Cassettes That Will Multiply Your Success!

Wisdom Is The Principal Thing
Tape Pak TS-18 / $30
Six Audio Tapes
The Wisdom Center

This life changing and revolutionary teaching is based on the Wisdom and The Principles of other champions in the Word of God. You will discover the greatest Wisdom Keys on earth and will begin unlocking the treasure containing every desired gift and miracle you are pursuing.

ORDER TODAY! 1-888-WISDOM-1
www.thewisdomcenter.cc (1-888-947-3661)

THE WISDOM CENTER • P.O. Box 99 • Denton, TX 76202